Missing on Mars

T0337575

Written by Narinder Dhami

Illustrated by Kyle Beckett

Collins

Red Town

Burning Lagoon

3

Reds never go to Pink Town.

Pinks never go to Red Town.

Zoom looks for earwigs.

Shimmer feeds a cow.

Zoom forgets to be back by dark.

The sun disappears. The moon appears.

Shimmer forgets to be back by dark.

Zoom and Shimmer meet in the darkness.

Zoom feels upset.

Shimmer hugs Zoom.

They will wait until morning.

But then ... they see torchlight!

Zoom sees Shimmer is red.

Shimmer sees Zoom is pink.
Wow! It is a shock!

Mars mail

Zoom and Shimmer meet in the dark!

Zoom and Shimmer

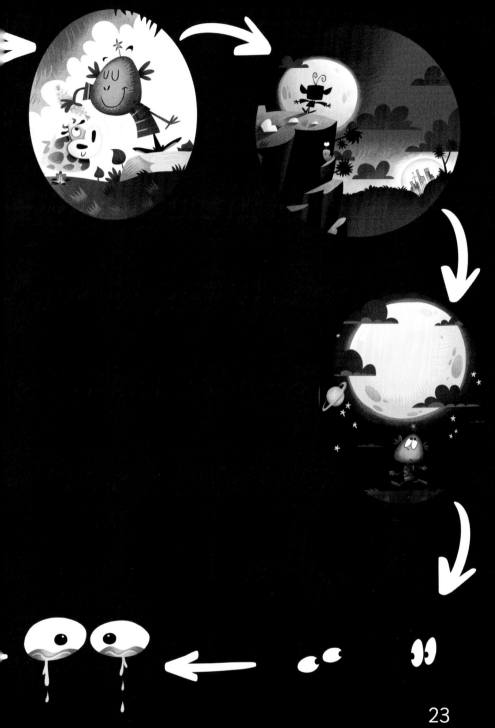

🐾 Review: After reading 🐾

Use your assessment from hearing the children read to choose any GPCs, words or tricky words that need additional practice.

Read 1: Decoding

- On page 6, point to the word **avoid**. Discuss its meaning. (e.g. *stay/keep away from*) Encourage the children to consider the word in the context of the sentence. (e.g. *be careful – don't go to Red Town*)
- Focus on the words with long vowels, beginning on pages 6 and 7. Ask the children which word ends in /er/. (**Shimmer**) and which has the /ow/ sound. (**Town**)
- Ask the children to find the digraphs and trigraph that make each of these sounds on pages 6–10:
  /ar/ (**dark**)   /oo/ (**Zoom**)   /oi/ (**avoid**)   /ear/ (**earwigs**)   /ee/ (**feeds**)
- Model reading pages 10 and 11, sounding out the words as you go. Next, reread the pages fluently. Challenge the children to read the pages fluently too. Say: Can you blend in your head when you read the words?

Read 2: Prosody

- Model reading pages 10 and 11 in a storyteller voice to create atmosphere and excitement. Explain that at this point, we don't know what will happen. Say: Zoom might end up in Red Town!
- Challenge the children to read the pages. Ask: How scary and worrying can you make the story sound?

Read 3: Comprehension

- Ask: What do you think Mars is really like? Why?
- Reread pages 4 and 5 and look at the pictures. Ask: What do the Reds think of the people in Pink Town, and what do the Pinks think of the people in Red Town? (e.g. *that they are frightening*)
- Turn to pages 22 and 23 and point to the pictures set in the dark. Ask:
  - How did Zoom and Shimmer get to be in the dark? (e.g. *they went out and forgot to be home by dark*)
  - What happens in the dark? (*Shimmer hugs Zoom because Zoom is upset*)
  - How do they feel when they see each other – why? (e.g. *They feel shocked because they each thought the other town's people were scary*)
- Bonus content: Look at pages 20 and 21, and discuss who the newspaper reporter might interview for the article. (e.g. *Shimmer and Zoom, and both their parents*) Encourage children to hot-seat each character and explore their feelings by answering "How did you feel when … ?" questions.